BIOLOGY Field Notes

Be an **ANT** Expert

by
Noah Leatherland

BEARPORT
PUBLISHING

Minneapolis, Minnesota

Credits

All images are courtesy of Shutterstock.com, unless otherwise specified. With thanks to Getty Images, Thinkstock Photo, Adobe Stock, and iStockphoto.

Recurring – Milano M, The_Pixel, Sonia Goncalves, Teguh Mujiono, sycomore, vectorplus. Doctor Character throughout – NotionPic. Cover – Eric Isselee, fotohunter. 4–5 – Achkin, Purino. 6–7 – Paulrommer SL, Pavel Krasensky. 8–9 – Bastiaan Schuit, Maytee Laohamaytee. 10–11 – Tirisphoto1, Mountains Hunter, GraphicsRF.com. 12–13 – Pavel Krasensky, Vinicius R. Souza. 14–15 – Andrey Pavlov, Andrey Pavlov, Jeremy Christensen. 16–17 – Nalinkarn Sakuljaroenying, winnond, jirasak_kaewtongsorn, frank60. 18–19 – dba87, ondrejprosicky. 20–21 – Tomatito, Pavel Krasensky. 22–23 – Andrey Pavlov, Anna in Sweden.

Bearport Publishing Company Product Development Team

President: Jen Jenson; Director of Product Development: Spencer Brinker; Managing Editor: Allison Juda; Associate Editor: Naomi Reich; Associate Editor: Tiana Tran; Art Director: Colin O'Dea; Designer: Kim Jones; Designer: Kayla Eggert; Product Development Assistant: Owen Hamlin

Library of Congress Cataloging-in-Publication Data

Names: Leatherland, Noah, 1999- author.
Title: Be an ant expert / by Noah Leatherland.
Description: Minneapolis, Minnesota : Bearport Publishing Company, [2025] |
  Series: Biology field notes | Includes index.
Identifiers: LCCN 2023059781 (print) | LCCN 2023059782 (ebook) | ISBN
  9798889169628 (hardcover) | ISBN 9798892324816 (paperback) | ISBN
  9798892321174 (ebook)
Subjects: LCSH: Ants--Juvenile literature. | Ants--Behavior--Juvenile
  literature.
Classification: LCC QL568.F7 L43 2025 (print) | LCC QL568.F7 (ebook) |
  DDC 595.79/615--dc23/eng/20240125
LC record available at https://lccn.loc.gov/2023059781
LC ebook record available at https://lccn.loc.gov/2023059782

For more information, write to Bearport Publishing, 5357 Penn Avenue South, Minneapolis, MN 55419.

CONTENTS

MEET THE BIOLOGIST

Hello! My name is Dr. Anthony Hill, and I am a **biologist**. I have traveled the world to learn all I can about ants. They are amazing **insects**!

Being an ant **expert** is a lot of work. I filled this notebook with everything I know about ants. Will you read it? Together, we can find out even more!

AN ANT'S BODY

There are more than 10,000 different kinds of ants. Like all insects, ants have six legs and three main body parts.

Ant Body Parts

Head

Thorax (THOR-aks)

Abdomen

Ants do not have bones. Instead, each ant has a hard covering called an **exoskeleton** on the outside of its body.

An exoskeleton keeps an insect's body safe.

SENSE AND CARRY

On the top of an ant's head are two long, thin body parts called **antennae** (an-TEN-ee). Ants use their antennae to feel, touch, smell, and taste the world around them.

Ants also use their antennae to share information with one another.

Antennae

8

In the front of their heads, ants have strong jaws called mandibles (MAN-duh-buhlz). These are used to grab onto food or to carry things. Ants also use their mandibles to fight.

One kind of ant can close its mandibles 2,300 times faster than you can blink!

Mandibles

9

THE ANT COLONY

Ants live in large groups called colonies. The insects in the colony work together. Most colonies have anywhere from a few hundred to many thousands of ants.

Tunnel

Chamber

Most ant colonies make their homes by digging underground. These nests have many small tunnels running between open spaces called chambers.

An anthill

The dirt taken out of the ground to build a nest creates an anthill.

QUEEN ANTS

Every ant colony has at least one queen. Queen ants are the only ants that lay eggs.

Queen ant

Ant eggs

Some queen ants can lay hundreds of eggs every day.

Can you guess which ant is the queen?

Queens are often the largest ants in a colony. They usually live deep inside the nests. Other ants help keep the queen safe.

ANT JOBS

In addition to queen ants, there are three other kinds of ants in a colony.

Workers

Worker ants do the work in the colony. Some workers take care of eggs and baby ants. Others leave the nest to find food for the colony. Still other workers take care of the queen.

Most of the ants in a colony are workers.

Soldiers

Soldiers keep the colony safe from hungry animals or enemy ants.

Soldier ants are a kind of worker ant. But they have much larger heads and mandibles.

Drones

Drones are winged ants that help the queen make more eggs.

TEAMWORK

Ants may be tiny, but together they can do amazing things. Some kinds of ants form bridges with their own bodies. Others hold on to one another to float on water or to carry food.

Ants are very strong for their size.

Ants following a smell trail

As they work together, ants **communicate** using smells. The insects leave trails of smells that tell about food or where the colony is. Other ants use their antennae to understand what the smells mean.

DINNERTIME

Ants are not picky about their food. The hungry insects will eat seeds, leaves, fruit, and tree sap. They also feast on small animals, such as other insects, some birds, fish, and lizards.

But ants also have to avoid becoming food!
Birds, lizards, and spiders often eat the insects.
Anteaters use long tongues to reach deep
inside anthills looking for a tasty treat.

An anteater

Sometimes, ants even eat other ants!

LIFE CYCLE

Baby ants are known as **larvae** (LAHR-vee). They hatch from the queen's eggs. The babies soon change to young ants called **pupae** (PYOO-pee). Workers give the pupae a lot to eat. Soon, they grow into adults.

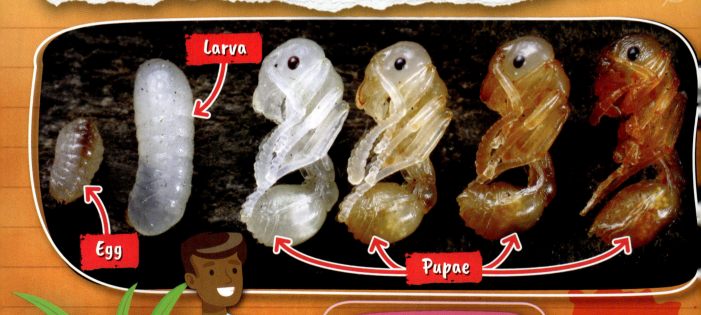

Larva

Egg

Pupae

A life cycle includes the different stages of an animal's life.

Young queens are called princess ants. They fly off and start their own colonies.

The biggest larvae become queens. The other young ants grow into drones, soldiers, or workers. Queens can live for up to 30 years, but most other ants have much shorter lives.

AWESOME ANTS

Although they are small, ants are awesome! I hope you've enjoyed learning about these amazing insects.

You have just begun your ant adventure. There is so much more to learn about them. Continue to study. Soon, you'll be an expert, too!

23

GLOSSARY

antennae the two long, thin body parts on the heads of insects

biologist a person who studies and knows a lot about living things

communicate to share information

exoskeleton the hard covering on the outside of an insect's body

expert a person who knows a lot about something

insects animals with six legs, three body parts, and a hard covering

larvae the legless baby forms of ants and other insects

pupae the young forms of ants and other insects

INDEX